ADDAE'S JOURNEY

- H. JAMES WILLIAMS -

ADDAE'S JOURNEY

Copyright © H. James Williams

Cover and Graphic Design by H. James Williams

ISBN-10: 0983434220

ISBN-13: 978-0983434221

LCCN: 2012910420

TABLE OF CONTENTS

Addae's Beginning 1

The Path of the Circle 9

The Path of the S-Curve 15

Triangular Awareness 21

v

ACKNOWLEDGMENT

The author wishes to acknowledge the divine nature of creation and its essence in all things.

DEDICATION

Addae's Journey is dedicated to teachers, mentors and advisers everywhere who enrich and nourish the human spirit within mankind for good purpose and the pursuit of individual excellence.

ADDAE'S BEGINNING

Addae (ah-DAH-eh) was a shy and withdrawn young boy who had his own way of taking in the world around him. He was not a precocious boy, but was discerning of people and nature. He took in most things in passing that others only tended to give a glancing eye. He was quick to notice a ray of sunshine, the way it glistened upon the iridescent colors of a butterfly's wing or to notice a droplet of dew formed upon a single leaf of grass. He was a child with a gentle spirit who appreciated the kindness of others. He was a child innocent in nature as was expected for any child his age.

Addae was an only child and had parents who nurtured and supported him with love. At 9 years old, Addae sensed that he was somehow different than other children. He was not a child who was in anyway self-centered or focused on himself in a negative way. He was a child who sometimes felt out-of-place and uncertain within himself about his earthly existence. He was not cognizant enough as yet to realize that he presently, and temporarily, lacked confidence in himself as a student of life much like first learning to swim, ride a bicycle or roller skate. Addae felt frail as an individual when he compared himself with his elementary schoolmates. Addae wanted to feel acceptance about himself. Even more so, he needed to discover confidence as moral fiber for ascent into his destined manhood.

Addae wondered why other children his age often seemed to know and understand more and to grasp learning faster than himself. At school, other children readily seemed to grasp what was being taught while he felt stifled and delayed in comprehending the same lessons. He was not a child that neglected his homework or who did not attempt to apply himself to learning. Addae instinctively knew that for him learning, and life's lessons, did not come as easy as it did for other children his age. He succumbed to his realization that he did not have the instant capacity for learning as did most other children. He had to apply himself with more effort, and more time, to master most subjects being taught to him.

One day a gentleman tall in stature, who seemed to Addae to be around the same age as Addae's grandparents, visited Addae's classroom to discuss the importance of education and learning in preparing for life and the future. He talked about the wonders of science, the healing properties of medicine, the poetry of language, the melody of music and the importance of learning what was being taught each day to step into the dreams and aspirations of tomorrow. Comparing building blocks to stepping stones of knowledge in life, he spoke of each day in

3

the classroom, and in life, as offering a building block of knowledge to be purposely and strategically placed in building your personal skyscraper into the future of tomorrow's possibilities. He explained that to waste any day of learning would be like tossing a stepping stone of knowledge onto a useless pile of rubble with no intended purpose. The children in the classroom all became increasingly inspired and excited about what education held for each of them and their futures. The gentleman, as with someone holding many keys for locked doors, answered each of their questions about their, as yet, unopened doors of tomorrow.

Although Addae was shy and withdrawn, when the questions by the other children had ceased, he timidly raised his hand to ask the gentleman a question. The man noticed Addae's shy demeanor and timid hand in the back of the classroom and with a perplexing sense of curiosity gave Addae the opportunity to pose his question. Addae was soft-spoken but deliberate in asking what he wished to learn and needed to know. The classroom fell silent. He asked the gentleman, "But what if you are not as smart as other children or as capable to learn and have a chance to make your dreams come true?" The other children, along with Addae, looked to the gentleman for his reply. The gentleman seemed ill-equipped to answer Addae, but with a pause and sudden revelation of thought, the gentleman struck upon an answer. Rather than answer Addae directly, the gentleman engaged the classroom to assist him in painting a picture of a response.

The gentleman asked the class to imagine a barren field without any vegetation or organic life. He then asked them to imagine a handful of seeds being cast about upon a stretch of the field's barren soil. He instructed and demonstrated for them to raise their arms and slowly lower their arms in front of them as they wiggled their fingers in the process. As the children did so, he asked them to pretend that their wiggling fingers were drops of rain falling to the ground moistening the soil upon which each drop landed. After a brief pause, he asked them to raise their arms again and slowly lower their arms to their sides in an arc as he also demonstrated. As they imitated him, he asked them to imagine their descending arms to be magical rays of sunshine radiating warmth and energy over the moistened soil. After pausing again, he began a mind quest for the children's personal discovery of an answer to Addae's question.

The gentleman began by quizzing Addae and the children about what would happen to the seeds after their exposure to the soil's nourishment, the rain's moisture and the sun's radiant warmth. The children's responses began. "The seeds would sprout roots and stems." "The stems would grow branches and leaves." "Flowers would begin to blossom." The gentleman then began another series of questions, "Would all of the seeds sprout roots and stems at the same time?" The children responded in unison with a drawn out, "Nooooooo." "Would all the stems develop branches, leaves and flowers at the same time?" "Nooooooo." "Would all of the plants and flowers grow to become the same height, size or color?" "Nooooooo." The gentleman then fully directed his attention to Addae. Addae he said, "You are like one of those flowers. Your flower may not grow and blossom at the same rate or pace as the flowers of the other children in your classroom, but your flower will grow and blossom into the flower you are meant to become someday. In the meantime, continue to do your best in school regardless of how much smarter anyone else may seem to be for the moment. Their flowers may presently be blossoming a little faster than yours, but this does not mean that their flowers will be any bigger or smaller than yours at the same time or at maturity. The **Spirit of Creation** will continually define for you purpose and meaning in your life if you

7

will allow yourself to remain attuned to its presence in your life. " He asked Addae if he understood. Addae smiled with a sense of confidence that he had not before felt. "Yes," he replied. Addae now understood that he would develop into his dreams and destiny, not at a pace defined by others or of his own making, but as he was able to innately develop, mature and apply himself with the best of his flowering ability. Addae went on to become an accomplished student and finished college with an advanced engineering degree while some of his other classmates, who once displayed great promise, either dropped out of school or were unable to finish school because of circumstances beyond their immediate control.

As a young man with academic credentials and a promising career, Addae felt that somehow there were still lessons for him to learn from life. He remembered the gentleman's advice that the **Spirit of Creation** would define purpose and meaning for him if he remained attuned to its presence in his life.

THE PATH OF THE CIRCLE

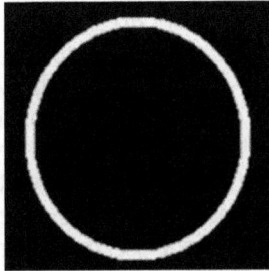

Addae had become an architectural engineer and at age 28 had been put in charge of a sizable engineering project at a major engineering firm. In becoming an engineer, he remembered the lesson to continually apply himself and learn each day's lesson presented to him. He felt blessed to have had many great teachers, mentors and persons of inspiration to guide him to this point in his life. He had become an architectural engineer because he liked the notion that just like in nature, creation engineers the structure of all animate and inanimate things. As an architectural engineer, he liked creating and designing structures and watching them proceed from an imaginary concept into a construction of reality. He had become very much attuned to the fact that whatever created mankind also created mankind with the ability to create as well. Savoring this truth, he appreciated that anyone's dreams, with clear purpose and determination, could be harnessed into meaningful reality.

The project Addae was now working on had encountered an engineering problem and setback that he could not seem to resolve or develop an engineering solution. He was frustrated and felt powerless to remedy the problem. He found himself going in circles with the same data trying to attempt a break-through to keep the project on track and meet its deadline. There seemed to him to be no immediate solution or remedy in sight. One day while having lunch with a senior engineering executive, he expressed his frustration. The senior executive looked at him and smiled. Addae wondered what could be so amusing about what he had expressed to the executive. The executive then spoke and said, "You are merely wandering in a circle on the path of your quest." He explained to Addae that once he stopped traveling the same circular path, in the same circular direction, he would come upon an appropriate exit to a solution.

After lunch Addae went back to his project and dwelled on the executive's advice. He threw out his old assumptions and paradigms about the project and also invited fresh thinking from his trusted colleagues and staff to bear upon the problem. He held focus groups and did benchmarking analysis of the best completed engineering projects in his field. In short time, a solution to the problem was arrived at and the project was successfully completed within budget and on time. Addae learned a valuable life lesson from this experience. He realized that life's journey is composed of circular paths that sometimes hinder our way. He thought about the biblical account of the Israelites traveling over desert in an endless circle until finding the way to their promised land. He now understood that at times in life we wander into the desert of idle efforts before stepping onto paths leading to opportunities of promise.

Addae was able to clarify for himself that sometimes we end up experiencing reoccurring circumstances in life because we remain in the endless rut of a circular path until we discover the lesson, or lessons, needed for exit to our next round of personal evolvement. He surmised that life is a journey with many sacred lessons. He could clearly see now that in many instances we have to repeat certain life lessons until we have learned the lessons meant to be learned before being able to exit its path for further enlightenment. Addae came to refer to this observation as

The Path of the Circle necessary in life for self-discipline and enlightenment to reach limitless heights of possibility and the reality of future dreams.

THE PATH OF THE S-CURVE

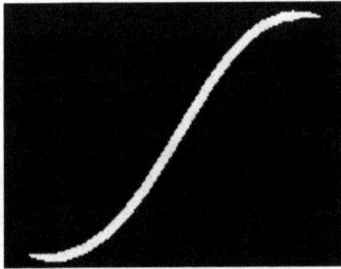

The success of several engineering projects that Addae had been put in charge of had brought him much favorable attention. He was respected near and far as a learned and responsible engineer within the engineering community. He was now 35 years old, had a lovely wife named Asha (AH-shah) and two adoring children: a son named Akil (ah-KEEL) and a daughter named Nyah (n-yah). Together, he and Asha had constructed a beautiful home and life together. He and Asha were comfortable and content with their accomplishments thus far in life.

Changes were taking place in the national economy and companies were reorganizing to better perform in the global market place. The company Addae worked for was no different. Employees who wished to remain employed by the company found themselves having to accept reassignments. Addae was asked to step into a leadership position at the company. He was not comfortable doing so. He did not wish to be responsible for the work of others, training others, leading others or managing others. He enjoyed, and was very happy, being assigned to oversee company projects. If Addae wanted to remain employed with the company, which he very much enjoyed working for, he would have to accept the management position he had been offered and also relocate his family. He discussed his situation with Asha and his children and reluctantly the decision was made to accept the position and its new responsibilities.

Addae received training in leadership and training on how to be an effective manager. He learned that there was a difference between merely controlling others to accomplish work versus inspiring and empowering others to accomplish work. He learned about organizational theory and human behavior. To his surprise, he enjoyed what he was learning and it helped him to be a better husband, a better father and to better interact with others in his new community. He became a very successful leader and manager and substantially improved the performance of the department he had been assigned to manage. He also had overcome his shyness about giving presentations and making impromptu speeches. His wife and children loved their new home and had adapted well to their new neighborhood and surroundings.

Addae, after many months, realized that

he had learned another lesson in life that he coined *The Path of the S-Curve* needed to keep from becoming too comfortable in life in order to explore and
prepare for new vistas of possibilities and reality. He realized that he had previously stopped growing as an individual and had not faced any new significant challenges that stretched him as an individual. He realized that in life we often reach plateaus of comfort and success that leave us stagnant and unmotivated to try new things and pursue new and worthwhile goals. If not mindful, we can come to rest upon our laurels of the moment and soon become outdated for purpose and meaning. He learned that life is continually about change and that if we are to grow as individuals, we have to adjust to change as necessary when confronted with circumstances sent our way in life to develop us for whatever purpose, or purposes, intended.

What he also learned from managing and overseeing engineering projects was that just like with projects, as in pursuits of life, there is an initiation phase, a planning phase, an execution/controlling phase and a closure phase. The closure phase of any project, or life challenge, is usually followed by the approach of a new beginning or challenge that awaits with its own S-Curve and accompanying developmental phases. Life for him now was like a series of oceanic waves to be surfed until it was time to surf the crest of the next oncoming wave of uncertainties and possibilities.

Addae gave his employer many years of loyal service and excelled to great height in the company. He had gained experience and confidence to set out on a wave he had not before dreamed of or had earlier in life anticipated. With the company's blessing, the support of the community and benefactors, he launched his own architectural engineering firm. Over time his firm and business grew and he was able to offer substantial employment to many people in his community as well as offer educational opportunities and internships to young students entering the architectural engineering field. He found himself being especially mindful to be on the lookout to assist students needing that little extra nudge to give themselves the confidence to fully pursue their dreams. He was now 49 years old and Akil and Nyah were attending universities of higher learning. His and Asha's parents were happily retired and life for he and Asha was indeed good. He and Asha were at the height of life's bell-curve journey.

Triangular Awareness

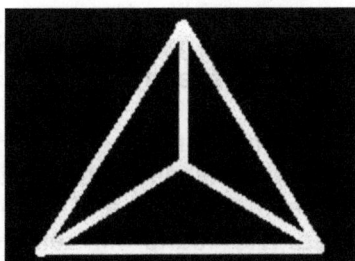

Addae found himself now longing for something different in his life that perplexed him. He could not fathom or understand what was troubling the very essence of his existence. He researched different venues of thought to gain insight to define what he felt was taking place within him. He wrestled with what was interfering with his self-actualization as an individual. He had worked and achieved an enviable position in life with accompanying income to provide for his family. He had honed and refined his potential for success and married the woman of his dreams. His wife and children were happy and pursing their own sense of purpose in life. He was respected in the community, gave to charities and paid homage to his faith.

Throughout Addae's life, he had projected and assigned meaning to situations, circumstances, objects and people he encountered. He found himself resigned and acceptant of what he could now not prescribe any meaning to, or purpose for, in his life.

One night, as he lay asleep, he was suddenly awakened by a lucid dream. The dream in every way seemed real and unimagined. In the dream he was a young boy again. He was not the shy boy he was as a child but was full of curiosity and wonder. He found himself sitting with a gentleman under a towering oak tree. The tree was rooted alongside a running brook that flowed from a mountain stream in the distance. The sun was shining down on the crest of the mountain causing the stream to glisten with radiant rays of light. He and the man did not speak in the dream. He and the man just seemed to share a time of clairvoyance and reciprocal thought. Turning to look more intently upon the man's face, he slowly recognized and remembered the man. The man was the tall gentleman who had visited his elementary school classroom. He remembered the man telling him to do his best and that the **Spirit of Creation** would continually define meaning and purpose for life. Suddenly, with keen sagacity, Addae remembered with clearer distinction that the man had specifically told him, "The **Spirit of Creation** will continually define for you purpose and meaning in your life if you will allow yourself to remain attuned to its presence in your life." The man, recognizing the clarity that had come upon Addae, rose to his feet. Addae, in like manner, stood also. The man then looked upon Addae with an approving smile and embraced

23

him in wisdom, kindness and love. Afterwards, the man slowly faded from sight leaving Addae's thirst for inner--peace and fulfillment quenched. It was at this point that Addae had awakened from his dream.

As Addae lie awake, he reflected upon what seemed to him an epiphany. He had followed the conviction of his dreams and possibilities for success in life and had become materially successful. However, he had not focused on the goodness of the spiritual dimension of himself beyond paying homage to his faith. He now understood that within him there was a higher-self, or consciousness, that also required spiritual growth and fulfillment. He shared his dream, and its perceived meaning for him, with Asha and afterwards with Akil and Nyah.

Over the following years, Addae found renewed strength from not placing too much focus and attention on material things in this life. He appreciated with greater clarity that he had not created himself and that he had been designed and created for meaningful purpose. As an engineer, he knew that things were not created in a vacuum but were created for a purpose and to serve a useful function. Addae now focused more intently on acknowledging that which managed the divine order of things within the universe. He knew that many called this essence by many names, but he simply knew this essence as **God**. He was now more deeply connected with the **Spirit of Creation** that dwelled within him for goodness. What he came to discover about this dimension of himself, he fondly called *Triangular Awareness*.

Triangular Awareness served to remind him that firstly, he was physically born into this world with limited innate knowledge, perceptions and impulses about its existence. Secondly, his consciousness learned perceived facts through critical thinking and the impulses of his physical being. His mind learned perceived facts for adapting to, or fully adopting, life's prerequisites for his physical survival. Thirdly, there was now a full acknowledgement within him of that which supremely existed in the universe and permeated all things. For him that permeation was the **Spirit of Creation** that his consciousness and inner-voice inwardly needed to remain attune to in order to complete his harmonic balance of body, mind and spirit in his earthly environment.

Addae was now complete and whole within himself. He had discovered unique aspects of the physical, mental and spiritual parts of himself that respectively remained in daily need of proper nourishment and care for personal wellbeing and growth. He had discovered a balance in life. He had discovered that physically, mentally and spiritually, he was connected to, and consisted of being a small part of, a larger universal whole. He had been uniquely engineered and constructed in **God's** image but he could only see and touch the presence of **God** in spirit. Through sincere prayer and earnest invocation, **God** permeated his spatial surroundings and secured him with clarity, guidance and personal fortitude for living.

EPILOGUE

Addae knew that he had become rich in far greater ways than just possessing money and material things. He was fortunate in life to have become rich in love and spirit. He remembered so many years ago when, as a shy little boy, he had dared to ask a gentleman visiting his classroom about learning capacity. He pondered now his blossoming into manhood and wisdom that could not be seen through the eyes of his boyhood. Thinking about his life's journey up to now, he scribbled the following poetic note to himself:

Sometimes we do not fully understand
  the journey ahead
Or how we will make it over the next mountain pass.
Sometimes the path before us seems without meaning,
*But the flowers along our way blossom with **His** promises.*

Sometimes our way grows dark
  with clouds of dismay,
And we find ourselves seemingly lost
  in the darkness of night.
But the sun always reappears to restore
  and brighten our faith,
*And **His** stars, with the moon,*
  illuminate our darkest hours with hope.

From the cradle we learn to walk
  and often stumble and fall.
Life at every bend and brook,
Presents its challenges that come to try our souls.
Trials and circumstances we all face;
  many of our own making,
*But **His** loving kindness and mercy*
  we count on to lift us when we fall.

Many have gone before us
  who while here extended a helping hand.
What hand do we extend to others
  attempting to make their way?
*We are all connected in the oneness of **His** spirit.*
To the least of any we extend a helping hand,
  *we extend **His** hand of love.*

Life on earth is a sacred journey
  to refine our souls for a life divine and without end.

The temples housing our souls
  are but chrysalides for heavenly transformation.

When we reach the end of this life's
  toilsome, mortal journey,
Life begins anew if we have been transformed
  *by **His** spirit and loving grace.*

Addae and Asha lived out the rest of their lives knowing that beyond this life's S-Curve another journey awaited each of them that is humanly indescribable. Nonetheless, they were confident that their **God,** the **Creator of All Things** would ultimately make the journey beyond this life accessible and known to them.

31

ABOUT THE AUTHOR

H. James Williams is s Certified Personal Coach and owner of Aliant Coaching Services in Baltimore, Maryland. He professionally administers personal coaching and interpersonal conflict mediation sessions and services. He is the author of *The Love Garden, Wavelets of Purpose* and *Love Pebbles.*

More information and other offerings can be obtained on the worldwide web at:

http://www.aliantsecuritygroup.org/